Let's Go to the Shops!

By Cameron Macintosh

It's fun to go to the shops with Mum and Dad.

You can go to the shops on a bus!

At the shops, you can get a cap.

This cap fits Dad well!

Mum can get a top
at the shops, too.

This top fits Mum well!

You can get a mug
in a shop.

This mug has a shell on it!

When you go to the shops, you can get choc chip buns.

What a yum bun!

At the shops, Shep can get a fun wig.

Look at Shep in this wig!

You can get a chess set at the shops.

Mum and I like chess.

When I go to the shops,
I get hot chips!

Yum, yum!

CHECKING FOR MEANING

1. What did Dad get at the shops? *(Literal)*

2. Which bun at the shops was yum? *(Literal)*

3. Where do you think Shep might wear her wig? *(Inferential)*

EXTENDING VOCABULARY

shop	What are words that can come before *shop* to tell you what can be bought at the shop? E.g. shoe *shop*, book *shop*, bread *shop*.
chess	Which words can you use to describe the *chess* board and the *chess* pieces? E.g. black, brown, carved, squares.
chips	Look at the word *chips*. What is the initial sound in this word? Find another word in the book that has the same sound at the start of the word.

MOVING BEYOND THE TEXT

1. What do you know about the game of chess? How is it played? How many players are there?

2. What is your favourite shop? What can you buy there? How does your family get to the shops?

3. What games do you like to play with your family?

4. What is your favourite food to buy at the shops? Why?

SPEED SOUNDS

| sh | ch | th | th | wh | qu | ph |

voiced   unvoiced

PRACTICE WORDS

This

shops

shell

choc

shop

chip

Shep

this

chess

When

chips